Aurora Gallery

The Pushkin Museum of Fine Arts

MOSCOW

PAINTING

AURORA ART PUBLISHERS · LENINGRAD

Text and catalogue
by TATYANA PRILUTSKAYA

Translated from the Russian
by ALEXIA BLOCH and LEIF TOMASSON

Designed by ILDUS FARRAKHOV

Layout by VALERY MATETSKY

Edited by VALERIA GUSEVA

The history of the Pushkin Museum of Fine Arts in Moscow is closely linked with the development of social thought and culture in Russia over the last three centuries. The idea of establishing an art museum was first put forward in the mid-eighteenth century by professors at the newly founded Moscow University. In 1831, two professors, Stepan Shevyriov and Mikhail Pogodin, began work on a project, backed by Princess Volkonskaya, herself a writer and patron of the arts; they received the support of the more progressive members of the Moscow aristocracy and of the intelligentsia. However, in the reactionary atmosphere which prevailed following the suppression of the Decembrists' uprising in 1825, the tsarist government opposed the founding of the museum. "The people need bread and shoes, not your museum," the Minister of Finance Sergei Witte told those responsible for the organization of the museum in 1895. The museum did not open until the beginning of the twentieth century, its acquisitions and construction funded by private donors, most notably by the industrialist Yuri Nechayev-Maltsev. A loyal supporter of the museum's founder Ivan Tsvetayev, he donated around 2.5 million roubles for the building of the museum.

The accumulation of works of art and the study of established European art-collecting traditions in Russia were linked with the increased importance of the arts at Moscow University. In 1816, a Numismatic Room was founded there and in 1848, a Room of Fine Arts and Antiquities, its first collection consisting of copies of famous classical sculptures. Subsequently, in 1857, a Department of Art History was founded. The most renowned and respected art critics and historians of the time — including such figures as Karl Hertz, Nikolai Romanov, Boris Turayev, Vladimir Malmberg, Victor Lazarev, Boris Vipper and many others — also contributed to the development of what was later to become the Pushkin Museum of Fine Arts.

The true founder of the museum, however, was the Moscow University professor Ivan Tsvetayev (1847—1931). The son of a poor village priest, he gained a world-wide reputation as a scholar, a renowned authority in the field of Latin philology. He belonged to that generation of the Russian intelligentsia which saw the greater purpose of their lives in the education and enlightenment of the people. In all, Tsvetayev dedicated twenty-five years of his life to creating the Museum of Fine Arts, bringing together the most outstanding scholars and artists.

At first the museum's collection consisted principally of copies of famous sculptures from all over the world. The collection was put together under the auspices of well-known museum specialists, including the famous scholar and director of the Berlin museums Wilhelm von Bode, the director of the Albertinum Museum in Dresden Georg Treu, the director of the Louvre Théophile Homolle, Professor Antonio Sogliano from Naples University and the director of the Egyptian Museum in Cairo, Heinrich Karl Brugsch.

In 1897, the Academy of Arts announced a contest for the design of the museum building. The winning project was created by the Moscow architect Roman Klein, who incorporated elements of ancient Oriental, Classical and Renaissance architecture into his Neoclassical design, the most striking feature of which is the stylistic unity of the interiors and the exhibits within them.

The Museum of Fine Arts, which now bears the name of the poet Alexander Pushkin, was opened to the public on 13 June (31 May, Old Style) 1912. Plaster duplicates of classical sculptures, ordered specially from the world's greatest museums, were exhibited in twelve halls. Several halls were devoted to European sculptures of the Middle Ages and Renaissance. These casts represented the first stage of the museum's development. However new perspectives in the museum's evolution were opening up. Thus, the museum acquired from the famous Russian egyptologist Vladimir Golenishchev an impressive collection of ancient Egyptian artefacts, comprising over 6,000 items. A new hall, decorated in the traditions of Egyptian temple architecture, was built to display them. In addition, the museum's reserves already owned 96 works by Italian and Italo-Cretan painters which had been donated to the museum in 1909 by the Russian diplomat Mikhail Shchokin.

The post-revolutionary reorganization of the museum marked a turning point in its history; the most significant event was the establishment of a picture gallery in 1924, the further development of which provides a vivid example of the new cultural policies of the Soviet government. In 1918, one of the first decrees of the Soviet government was issued, "On the prohibition of the export and sale abroad of objects of special artistic and historical significance". Another decree mandated the "acquisition, registration and safeguarding of objects of art and antiquity which are in the possession of private owners, associations and institutions". Numerous works of art from nationalized collections, the tsars' palaces and state institutions were combined to form a State Museum Fund from which museums in various cities could supplement their collections.

Paintings by Western European masters, bequeathed to the State for the "enlightenment of the people" by the chancellor of the Russian court, Count Nikolai Rumiantsev, at the turn of the nineteenth century, became the nucleus of the picture gallery. Rumiantsev also donated old manuscripts, historical documents, ethnographical and archaeological relics and books, which led to the creation of the Book and Manuscript Fund of the largest State library in Russia — the Lenin Library in Moscow. Among other "westernized Russians" who had put together significant collections in Russia were the Yusupovs, Shuvalovs, Stroganovs and Sheremetevs; works from these collections are now to be found in many museums in Moscow, Leningrad and other cities of the country.

The receipt in 1924 of 146 marvellous paintings by Netherlandish, Dutch, German and Italian masters was especially significant for the picture gallery. These paintings came from the private collection of Dmitry Shchukin, who was later appointed curator of the gallery's Italian department. A number of outstanding oil paintings, drawings and works of applied art were acquired by the museum from the estates and private residences of Russian aristocratic families such as the Gagarins, Meshcherskys and Bariatinskys, from the industrialists the Brokarts, Riabushinskys and Kharitonenkos, and from the reserves of the Historical Museum, the Kremlin Museums and the Tretyakov Gallery in Moscow.

On 11 November 1924 two new exhibition halls were opened, devoted to Netherlandish and German painting, and in the following year Italian, Spanish, Dutch and Flemish halls were added. Subsequent contributions from Leningrad museums, primarily the Hermitage, put the collection on a par with the world's greatest museums. Approximately 500 paintings by the world's most famous artists, including Perugino, Canaletto, Lucas Cranach the Elder, Rembrandt, Rubens, Poussin, Murillo and others, became part of the museum's permanent collection.

Further growth of the Pushkin Museum was interrupted by the outbreak of the Second World War. In 1941 the collections were transferred to cities in Siberia, but even during the worst years of the war the museum's curators organized exhibitions and lectures and cared for the remaining parts of the collections in the museum, which was partly destroyed by bombing. In October 1946, the building's pre-war layout was completely restored. At this time the staff carried out an extensive restoration of paintings from the Dresden Gemäldegalerie. These paintings had been found by Soviet soldiers in damp, mined shelters around Dresden, in desperate need of expert care. After their restoration they were put on display in the USSR and, in 1955, returned to Dresden.

In 1948, the picture gallery acquired yet another collection of paintings — 286 works, mainly by late nineteenth- and early twentieth-century French artists. The collection was transferred from the former Museum of Modern Western Art in Moscow, the holdings of which at that time were being distributed to various museums. These paintings had originally belonged to the famous Moscow art collectors Sergei Shchukin and Ivan Morozov.

Additions to the picture gallery continue today in the form of government purchases and donations by Russian and foreign collectors and artists. The list of prestigious donors includes the secretary and close friend of Henri Matisse, Lydia Delectorskaya; Fernand Léger's widow, Nadezhda Khodasevich-Léger; the collectors Mark Kaganovich and Baron Thyssen-Bornemisza; and the artists Rockwell Kent, Renato Guttuso, Armando Pizzinato, Diego Rivera, Alfaro Siqueiros, Francesco Messina and Emilio Greco. Government purchases over the last few years have added paintings by Emile-Antoine Bourdelle, Giacomo Manzù, Corneliu Baba, Zlatu Bojadgiev, and others.

The museum's collections now include over half a million works of art and cultural relics. Under the Soviet government, since 1917, the number of items has increased fifty times over. The museum organizes exhibitions of its new acquisitions every five years.

The most recent event in the museum's history was the organization, in 1987, of a special department, where pictures donated or bequeathed to the museum are put on display. To extend the exhibitions and to acquire additional room for concerts and scientific and educational activities several adjoining buildings dating from the sixteenth to nineteenth centuries were given to the museum. A department of engravings and drawings was also established, in 1966, in a small private residence built in the first quarter of the nineteenth century, an excellent example of Russian Neoclassical architecture which had been restored by the museum. At present the collection includes over 350,000 works of art by Russian, Soviet and foreign masters.

The museum regularly participates in exchanges with major museums throughout the world. One of the best illustrations of international collaboration was the well-known exhibition *Moscow — Paris: 1900—1930*, which first opened in the Georges Pompidou Centre in Paris in 1979 and then in 1981 came to the Pushkin Museum of Fine Arts in Moscow.

Today the museum is a renowned cultural and educational centre, visited by over a million people each year and sponsoring art-historical research and applied art clubs for young people. Aspiring towards a synthesis of all art forms, the museum annually gives over its premises to the now traditional music festival December Evenings. Musicians from many countries take part and the festival is accompanied by a specially organized exhibition.

The museum's exposition unfolds chronologically: it begins with sculptures and copies showing the art of the ancient world and the Middle Ages and rounds off with thirteenth- to twentieth-century paintings from Western Europe and America.

The exhibition of paintings begins with the collection of Fayum portraits, the earliest paintings from Graeco-Roman Egypt, and is continued by a small but exceptionally fine group of Byzantine icons from the fourteenth century, the last period of the flourishing of Byzantine culture. The icon of St Pantaleon stands out with its clear design and saturated colours, whilst *The Twelve Apostles* is also noteworthy for its noble, restrained colouring and subtle psychological nuances.

The onlooker can trace the brilliant course of Italian painting over the past five centuries. Monumental works, such as two versions of the *Madonna and Child Enthroned*, bear witness to the assimilation and reinterpretation of Byzantine traditions by Pisan and Florentine artists towards the end of the thirteenth century. The nobility, lyricism and elegant colours of these works, suffused with spiritual feeling, are characteristic of such Florentine, Sienese and Venetian masters of the Trecento as Lippo Memmi, Giovanni di Bartolommeo Cristiani, Sano di Pietro and Lorenzo Monaco.

The collection of paintings from the Italian Renaissance presents many of its facets, including works by lesser known masters. The two remaining parts of Botticelli's *Annunciation* polyptych can be singled out from other works of this period by their exalted feeling, their extraordinary refinement of form and the distinct expressiveness of the linear rhythm. The harmony and spirituality characteristic of High Renaissance masters is most brilliantly illustrated in Perugino's *Madonna and Child* and *St Sebastian* by Giovanni Antonio Boltraffio, one of the best of Leonardo da Vinci's many followers. Among the museum's large selection of Mannerist paintings are works by Giulio Romano, Giovanni Battista Naldini, Francesco Salviati and Lorenzo Lotto. Bronzino's remarkable *Holy Family with St John the Baptist*, with its cold virtuosity, is an excellent example of Mannerism. The small *Betrothal of St Catherine* by Parmigianino also merits special attention for the feeling of the illusory, unstable nature of objective reality which it communicates.

The area most fully represented in the Italian collection is the art of Venice. Cima da Conegliano's *Descent from the Cross* and *Christ Enthroned* display a remarkable combination of stately images with a depth and softness of colour. The best among the works by Veronese in the museum is the small sketch *Minerva*, with its iridescent colour and free manner of execution, from which one can easily trace a path to the fine artistry and watercolour-like translucency of the sketches, *Two Saints* and *The Death of Dido*, by Giovanni Battista Tiepolo, the eighteenth-century Venetian master of monumental paintings. Francesco Guardi's early and unusual work, *Alexander the Great and the Body of Darius*, is executed in the extravagant Baroque *maniera del tocco* and differs from the *plein-air* treatment of his small *capriccios*, *View of Venice* and *Courtyard in Venice*. In the rich collection of Venetian *vedute*, *The Betrothal of the Doge to the Adriatic Sea* by Canaletto (Antonio Canal) is notable for its luminous, vivid colours. The roots of Italian landscape painting and its connection with the traditions of the late Gothic panoramic views are apparent in the *Landscape with Scenes from the Lives of Saints* by the Ferrarese artist Dosso Dossi.

The variety of trends and aspirations seen in Italian painting in the seventeenth and eighteenth centuries is manifested in the works by artists of the academic school such as Lodovico Carracci and Guido Reni, by Caravaggio's followers Pier Francesco Mola and Domenico Fetti, and in the highly dramatic art of the Genoese masters, Bernardo Strozzi and Alessandro Magnasco.

The museum's collection of northern European paintings begins with late Gothic altarpieces by German and Austrian masters. *The Virgin and Child* and *The Effects of Jealousy* by Lucas Cranach the Elder, representative of the German Renaissance, are painted with meticulous precision. *The Flight into Egypt* by the Swabian master known as the Monogrammist AB dates from the same period and is distinctly national in character.

One of the museum's richest collections is that of sixteenth-century Netherlandish art. The highly finished detail and delicacy of Adriaen Isenbrant's *The Virgin and Child* and the contemplative and poetic character of the *Portrait of Anne, Duchess of Cleves* by an unknown early sixteenth-century master continue the best traditions of the Netherlandish school in the preceding century. This collection also includes landscapes by Herri met de Bles, Freudeman de Fris and Jan Brueghel the Elder, who worked later in the sixteenth century. Paintings such as Joachim Bueckelaer's *In the Marketplace*, Pieter Pietersz's *In the Fish Shop* and the two portraits by Adriaen Tomasz Key anticipate the diversity of genres in seventeenth-century Dutch and Flemish painting.

Among the seventeenth-century Flemish paintings, the place of honour has justly been given to the brilliant Peter Paul Rubens. We can assess the scope of his artistic endeavour in his marvellous oil sketch of a triumphal arch, *The Apotheosis of the Archduchess Isabella*, one of the famous series of decorations designed to mark the arrival in Antwerp of the Spanish governor-general of Flanders, the Cardinal Infante Ferdinand. Rubens's *Bacchanal* is a classical example of his consummate artistry: the powerful life-giving elements of nature seem to take on sensual full-blooded bodily form, further intensified by the rich golden tones. The Baroque naturalism and strong national overtones of Jacob Jordaens's canvases (*A Satyr in a Peasant House*), as well as the lavish colour and exuberance of Frans Snyders's still lifes (*Fish Shop*), show a debt to the Rubensian tradition, which stands in sharp contrast to the grotesque works, *Smoker* and *Jester*, by David Teniers the Younger and to Jan Siberechts's romantic landscape, *Ford*.

Seventeenth-century Dutch paintings were popular among Russian collectors from the time of Peter the Great, and the museum boasts works by the most celebrated artists of the time.

Among them are still lifes by such painters as Pieter Claesz, Willem Claesz Heda and Juriaen van Streeck. *Still Life with a Nautilus Shell Goblet* by Willem Kalf should be especially noticed for its noble and refined quality. The rich tonality of the finely harmonized colour scheme unites Adriaen van Ostade's dramatically grotesque peasant scenes and the poetic pictures of everyday life by Pieter de Hooch and Gerard Terborch. The full spectrum of expressive potential of Dutch landscape painting can be seen in the lyrical and contemplative *View of the Waal at Nijmegen* by Jan van Goyen, in the spacious *View in Gelderland* by Philips Koninck and in the dramatic *View of Egmond aan Zee* by Isaacksz van Ruisdael. The emotional perception of life as revealed by Emanuel de Witte's *Market in the Port*, painted in cold, clear colours, comes close to the work of the greatest of Dutch painters, Rembrandt Harmensz van Rijn.

The museum owns six paintings by Rembrandt, of which two, *Christ Driving the Money-changers from the Temple* and *The Incredulity of St Thomas*, date from his early period. A later *Portrait of Adriaen van Rijn* (?) (1654) shows profound psychological insight and the artist's perfect command of expressive means. The masterpiece *Ahasuerus, Haman and Esther* is distinguished by incredible emotional tension; the troubled atmosphere of conflicting feelings — of sorrow and anger, of inner doubt and resolution — is conveyed by fine gradations of colour applied in thick, shimmering impasto.

Certainly, the most complete and valuable section of the picture gallery is the exhibition of French paintings from the seventeenth to twentieth centuries, which begins with five paintings by Nicolas Poussin, the leading French seventeenth-century classicist. In his early work *The Victory of Joshua over the Amorites* the direct influence of Classical Antiquity and Italian Mannerism is still visible. Masterpieces from Poussin's early, "Titian", period include his *Satyr and Nymph*, with its refined elegance and transparent lightness of colour, and the renowned *Rinaldo and Armida*. The heroic landscape became the main focus of Poussin's creative endeavour in the later period of this career, and one of the best examples of this is the *Landscape with Hercules and Cacus*. The monumentality and severity of his paintings from this period echo the dramatic struggle of the eternal elements of the universe. The radiant landscape paintings *Battle on the Bridge* and *The Rape of Europa* by Poussin's contemporary Claude Gellée (Claude Lorrain) are of a more lyrical nature.

Other facets of French seventeenth-century art are expressed in the works of the Caravaggist Valentin (Jean de Boulogne), the Baroque painter Simon Vouet and the "masters of reality" of the circle around the Le Nain brothers. Among the museum's collection of formal portraits from the age of Louis XIV, Hyacinthe Rigaud's psychologically acute and intimate portrait of the writer and philosopher Fontenelle is of particular interest.

The brilliant art of France in the eighteenth century is represented by two early paintings by Antoine Watteau, *The Bivouac* and *Satire on Physicians*, imbued with a feeling of melancholy and irony. The artist's painterly manner is distinguished by whimsical dabs of the brush and by a wealth of transparent half-tones. The influence exerted by Watteau on his compatriots is apparent in the charming pastorals by masters of the *fêtes galantes* such as Jean-Baptiste Pater, Nicolas Lancret and Antoine Quillard. François Boucher's *Hercules and Omphale* reveals an astounding artistic temperament. It is painted with free, sweeping brushstrokes, rather in the tradition of Rubens, and differs sharply from the many other works by Boucher in the museum.

The museum's exposition of French paintings of the late eighteenth and early nineteenth centuries opens with Jacques-Louis David's small but extremely detailed sketch *Andromache Laments the Death of Hector*. For this work, completed in 1783, David was awarded the title of Academician. His *Self-portrait* and *Portrait of Ingres as a Young Man* (?), with their elevated painting manner, foreshadowed French Romanticism.

The grandiose and accentuated exotic nature of Antoine Jean Gros's ceremonial *Equestrian Portrait of Prince Boris Yusupov*, two small studies, one by Théodore Géricault (*Study of a Male Model*) and another by Eugène Delacroix (*After a Shipwreck*), are typical examples of fully developed Romanticism.

Echoes of Romanticism can be found in works from other European schools, for instance, in John Constable's freely painted *View of Highgate from Hampstead Heath* from the museum's collection of English art and in Caspar David Friedrich's *Mountainous Landscape*, which is representative of nineteenth-century German painting.

Along with the large collection of landscape views by masters of the French Barbizon school, special importance is attached to landscape paintings by Camille Corot, tracing the evolution of his style from the clarity and precision of his early *Morning in Venice* to the pearly haze of his later paintings, *Château de Pierrefonds* and *Stormy Weather*.

The most famous part of the French collection, however, is that of the Impressionists, Post-Impressionists and early twentieth-century masters of other trends who worked in France.

Among the paintings of Claude Monet, the leading figure of the Impressionism, *Luncheon on the Grass* merits special attention. This is a replica of a lost work, one of his first Impressionist experiments. Another remarkable painting is the programmatic canvas *The Boulevard des Capucines in Paris*, which was shown at the first Impressionist exhibition in 1874. The museum owns eleven paintings by Monet covering all stages of his artistic career and giving a comprehensive idea of the master's bold handling of light and colour. These works stand in contrast to the poetic vision and restrained colour of Camille Pissarro's landscapes and to the pure, perfectly arranged colours and compositional clarity of the paintings of Alfred Sisley.

Three works by Pierre Auguste Renoir date from the peak of the artist's creative activity — *Nude, Portrait of the Actress Jeanne Samary* and *Girls in Black*, replete with the exultant poetry of a fleeting mood. His other paintings in the museum include *In the Garden. Under the Trees of the Moulin de la Galette* and *Bathing on the Seine* (*La Grenouillère*), which combine a *plein-air* spontaneity and iridescent ornamental colouring.

The ballet and horse-race scenes by Edgar Degas are no less impressionistic in their cold, sharp communication of unexpected glimpses of contemporary life. *Dancer Posing for a Photographer*, painted in exquisite ash-grey tones, deals with a prosaic, commonplace motif, reflecting both mocking and a wistful understanding, but above all witnessing to Degas's impeccable artistic taste.

Among the fourteen works by the great revolutionary in painting Paul Cézanne is the famous *Still Life with Peaches and Pears*, which is seen as the artist's pictorial manifesto: the painting reflects Cézanne's integral perception of the surrounding world and his desire to translate onto canvas the most stable, essential qualities of objects, not influenced by the changing environment. Cézanne's early paintings as, for example, *The Road at Pontoise*, are very similar to Impressionist works in their colouring. *The Banks of the Marne* is a mature work, characterized by a classical harmony and balance which, in his later masterpieces such as *Landscape at Aix* (*Mont Sainte-Victoire*), succumbs to Cezánne's boisterous temperament and energy.

The museum's five paintings by Vincent van Gogh date from the last years of his life. In the *Portrait of Dr Rey* one can sense the alarming discord between the cold mask of the face, stylized in the traditions of Japanese art, and the tense pulsating rhythm of the ornamental background. *Landscape at Auvers after the Rain* is pervaded with melancholy and with admiration for the cleanness of the newly-washed countryside, softened by the parting glance of the dying artist. The flaming colour of the *Red Vineyard at Arles* transforms the conventional image into that of a cosmic catastrophe.

Among the museum's fourteen Gauguins the most remarkable is the bitter and ironic *Café at Arles* and the extremely interesting series of Tahitian paintings, including *Are You Jealous?*, *Gathering Fruit* and *The Flight* (*Ford*), in which the linear rhythm and exotic colour combinations unite the folklore traditions of non-European civilizations with the decorative devices of contemporary art.

The decorative reinterpretation of Impressionism at the turn of the century gave rise to the Pointillist technique with its bright enamel-like colour and texture, seen in paintings by Paul Signac, Henri-Edmond Cross and Henri Charles Manguin. The muted pastel colours in Pierre Bonnard's *Summer in Normandy* and *Early Spring in the Country*, intended for the decoration of Ivan Morozov's private residence in Moscow, and the intimacy of Jean Edouard Vuillard's interiors *In the Room* and *On the Sofa* also testify to these new tendencies.

The works of André Derain, Maurice de Vlaminck, Cornelis (Kees) van Dongen, Albert Marquet and Henri Matisse show their initial links with Fauvism and their later individual efforts. In the simplicity and skilfully organized colour scheme of Albert Marquet's *Harbour at Honfleur* and *Notre-Dame in Winter* one can feel new vistas opening for the traditional European landscape genre in the twentieth century. The museum also possesses paintings from André Derain's Gothic period, in which the ascetic colour and bare structure of form — as in his landscape paintings rendering the uncontrolled energy of natural forms — reflect the development of the expressive potential of Cubism.

The works of Henri Matisse and Pablo Picasso symbolize the peak of French twentieth-century artistic genius. The museum's eighteen paintings by Matisse came from the same source as the majority of the late nineteenth- and early twentieth-century works, namely, from the Shchukin and Morozov collections. In addition, Lydia Delectorskaya donated several of the artist's works and two of his own palettes to the museum. The paintings date mainly from the 1890s to the 1910s. The so-called Moroccan triptych is based on contrast: the refined

Oriental colouring of two of its parts (*Zorah on the Terrace* and *Entrance to the Casbah*), with the harmonious combination of turquoise-green and ruby-red tones, stands opposed to the clearly defined contrasts of light and shadow in the third part (*View from a Window. Tangier*). The almost watercolour transparency of the *Goldfish* and *Bouquet of Flowers in a White Vase* is juxtaposed with the rich, dense painting of *Fruit and Bronze*.

Eleven canvases by Pablo Picasso, painted between 1900 and 1912, present different stages in the evolution of his style. In the *Portrait of the Poet Jaime Sabartés*, *Family of Saltimbanques* and *Old Jew and a Boy* the theme of inevitable doom resounds with increasing intensity, the figures symbolically embodying the tragic fate of mankind. Picasso's major work from his Rose Period, *Girl on a Ball*, is one of his most poetic creations. The contrasts of its plastic and colouristic structures are overcome in the uneasy balance of strength and weakness, of alienation and spiritual links between people, and of hope and sorrow. His Cubist works *Queen Isabeau*, *Lady with a Fan*, *Portrait of Ambroise Vollard* and *Still Life with a Violin* reflect a collapsing world which is being reunited by the will and intellect of the artist to produce a new, conflict-laden pictorial reality.

The exhibition of twentieth-century art grows and changes regularly, incorporating works by Fernand Léger, Rockwell Kent, Diego Rivera and Renato Guttuso. The museum also displays paintings and sculptures by such artists as Zlatu Bojadgiev of Bulgaria, Corneliu Baba of Romania, Xawery Dunikowski of Poland and Bert Heller and Willy Sitte of Germany. The gallery continues to expand, aiming to present a broad and objective picture of world art.

Tatyana Prilutskaya

BYZANTINE MASTER OF THE FIRST THIRD
    OF THE 14TH CENTURY
FLORENTINE MASTER
    OF THE LATE 13TH CENTURY
GIOVANNI DI BARTOLOMMEO CRISTIANI
LIPPO MEMMI (?)
MASTER OF THE LIECHTENSTEIN CASTLE
PEDRO ESPALARGUES (?)
MONOGRAMMIST AB
LUCAS CRANACH THE ELDER
BOTTICELLI
DOSSO DOSSI
PERUGINO
PARMIGIANINO
BRONZINO
VERONESE
LODOVICO CARRACCI
GUIDO RENI
DOMENICO FETTI
BERNARDO STROZZI
PIER FRANCESCO MOLA
JOHANN LISS
ADRIAEN ISENBRANT
UNKNOWN NETHERLANDISH ARTISTS
    OF THE EARLY 16TH CENTURY
ADRIAEN TOMASZ KEY
PIETER PIETERSZ
ADRIAEN VAN OSTADE
ABRAHAM VAN BRYEREN (?)
WILLEM KALF
JACOB VAN GEEL
EMANUEL DE WITTE
GERARD TERBORCH
PHILIPS KONINCK
PIETER DE HOOCH
JURIAEN VAN STREECK
REMBRANDT HARMENSZ VAN RIJN
PETER PAUL RUBENS
ANTHONY VAN DYCK
FRANS SNYDERS
JACOB JORDAENS
DAVID TENIERS THE YOUNGER
JAN SIBERECHTS
FRANCISCO DE ZURBARÁN
BARTOLOMÉ ESTEBAN MURILLO
ALESSANDRO MAGNASCO
GIUSEPPE MARIA CRESPI
GIOVANNI BATTISTA TIEPOLO
MICHELE GIOVANNI MARIESCHI
FRANCESCO GUARDI

NICOLAS POUSSIN
CLAUDE GELLÉE
    (CLAUDE LORRAIN)
ANTOINE WATTEAU
HYACINTHE RIGAUD
ANTOINE QUILLARD
FRANÇOIS BOUCHER
JACQUES-LOUIS DAVID
ANTOINE JEAN GROS
THÉODORE GÉRICAULT
EUGÈNE DELACROIX
CASPAR DAVID FRIEDRICH
JOHN CONSTABLE
THOMAS LAWRENCE
CHARLES FRANÇOIS DAUBIGNY
NARCISSE DIAZ DE LA PEÑA
GUSTAVE COURBET
JEAN FRANÇOIS MILLET
JEAN-BAPTISTE CAMILLE COROT
PIERRE PUVIS DE CHAVANNES
JULES BASTIEN-LEPAGE
EUGÈNE BOUDIN
CLAUDE MONET
CAMILLE PISSARRO
ALFRED SISLEY
PIERRE AUGUSTE RENOIR
EDGAR DEGAS
VINCENT VAN GOGH
PAUL GAUGUIN
PAUL CÉZANNE
MAURICE DENIS
JEAN EDOUARD VUILLARD
PIERRE BONNARD
HENRI ROUSSEAU
PAUL SIGNAC
MAURICE UTRILLO
EDVARD MUNCH
IGNACIO ZULOAGA
ALBERT MARQUET
MAURICE DE VLAMINCK
ANDRÉ DERAIN
HENRI MATISSE
CORNELIS (KEES) VAN DONGEN
GEORGES ROUAULT
PABLO PICASSO
ROCKWELL KENT
FERNAND LÉGER
RENATO GUTTUSO
DECHKO UZUNOV
CORNELIU BABA

PLATES

1. BYZANTINE MASTER OF THE FIRST THIRD
OF THE 14TH CENTURY

The Twelve Apostles

Tempera on panel. 38×34 cm

2. FLORENTINE MASTER
OF THE LATE 13TH CENTURY. *Italy*

The Madonna and Child Enthroned. *C.* 1275—80

Tempera on panel. 246×138 cm

→

3. GIOVANNI DI BARTOLOMMEO CRISTIANI.
Mentioned between 1366 and 1398. *Italy*

The Madonna and Child with Angels

Tempera on panel. 164×92 cm

4. LIPPO MEMMI (?). Mentioned between 1317 and 1347. *Italy*
Mary Magdalene
Tempera on panel. 66×50 cm

5. MASTER OF THE LIECHTENSTEIN CASTLE. Active around 1440 in Vienna. *Austria*
The Nativity
Oil on panel, 101×50 cm

6. PEDRO ESPALARGUES (?). Active in the late 15th and early 16th centuries. *Spain*
The Archangel Michael Weighing the Souls of the Dead
Tempera on panel. 172×90 cm

7. MONOGRAMMIST AB. Active in the second
third of the 16th century in Swabia. *Germany*

The Flight into Egypt

Signed in a monogram, left, at the base of the column: *AB*
(the letter *B* has been changed for *D*)
Oil on panel. 43×39 cm

8. LUCAS CRANACH THE ELDER. 1472—1553.
Germany

The Virgin and Child. *C.* 1525

Oil on panel. 58×46 cm

→

9, 10. BOTTICELLI (ALESSANDRO DI MARIANO FILIPEPI). 1444/5—1510. *Italy*

The Annunciation. 1490s. Parts of an altarpiece

Tempera on canvas (transferred from panel). 45×13 cm (each part)

11. DOSSO DOSSI
(GIOVANNI DE LUTERI).
C. 1479—1542. *Italy*
**Landscape with Scenes
from the Lives of Saints**
Oil on canvas. 60×87 cm

12. PERUGINO (PIETRO VANNUCCI).
C. 1450—1523. *Italy*
The Madonna and Child. *C.* 1490
Oil on canvas (transferred from panel). 51×38 cm

13. PARMIGIANINO (FRANCESCO MAZZOLA).
1503—1540. *Italy*

The Betrothal of St Catherine

Oil on canvas. 21×29 cm

14. BRONZINO (AGNOLO DI COSIMO DI MARIANO).
1503—1572. *Italy*
The Holy Family with St John the Baptist
Oil on canvas (transferred from panel). 117×99 cm

15. VERONESE (PAOLO CALIARI).
1528—1588. *Italy*
Minerva. 1560s
Oil on canvas. 28×16 cm

16. LODOVICO CARRACCI. 1555—1619. *Italy*
The Holy Family under a Palm Tree
Oil on canvas. 41×29 cm

17. GUIDO RENI. 1575—1642. *Italy*
The Adoration of the Shepherds. *C.* 1642
Oil on panel. 100×100 cm (octagon)

18. DOMENICO FETTI. *C.* 1589—1623. *Italy*

David with the Head of Goliath

Oil on canvas. 105×81 cm

19. BERNARDO STROZZI (called IL PRETE GENOVESE
or IL CAPPUCCINO). 1581—1644. *Italy*

The Multiplication of Loaves and Fishes

Oil on canvas. 181×136 cm

20. PIER FRANCESCO MOLA. 1612—1666. *Italy*
Homer Dictating His Verses
Oil on canvas. 88×100 cm

27. PIETER PIETERSZ. 1540—1603. *The Netherlands*
In the Fish Shop. *C.* 1570
Oil on panel. 112×84 cm

26. ADRIAEN TOMASZ KEY.
C. 1544 — after 1589. *The Netherlands*

Portrait of a Woman. *C.* 1573

Signed in a monogram, bottom right, on the chair: *ATK*
Oil on panel. 101×72.5 cm

24, 25. UNKNOWN ARTIST
OF THE EARLY 16TH CENTURY. *The Netherlands*
St Crispin (?). Two Donors. Parts of an altarpiece
Oil on canvas (transferred from panel). 97.8 × 39.2 cm (each part)

23. UNKNOWN ARTIST. Active around 1500.
The Netherlands

Portrait of Anne, Duchess of Cleves

Oil on canvas (transferred from panel). 32.3×22.5 cm

22. ADRIAEN ISENBRANT. ?—1551.
The Netherlands
The Virgin and Child. Central panel of a triptych
Oil on panel. 50.3×35 cm

21. JOHANN LISS. *C.* 1597—*c.* 1630. *Germany*
The Flaying of Marsyas
Oil on copperplate. 49×37 cm

28. ADRIAEN VAN OSTADE. 1610—1685. *Holland*
A Tavern Scene. *C.* 1635
Signed and dated, bottom right: *A v Ostade 16*[...]
Oil on panel. 41×55 cm

29. ABRAHAM VAN BEYEREN (?).
1620/21—1690. *Holland*

Breakfast

Signed, right, on the table: *AB f*
Oil on panel. 74×60 cm

30. WILLEM KALF. 1619—1693.
Holland

Still Life with a Nautilus Shell Goblet. *C.* 1660

Oil on canvas. 76×62 cm

31. JACOB VAN GEEL. *C.* 1585—*c.* 1638.
Holland
Landscape with a Big Tree. First third
of the 17th century
Oil on panel. 41×56.5 cm

32. EMANUEL DE WITTE. 1616/17—1692. *Holland*
Market in the Port. 1660s
Oil on canvas. 60.7×75.5 cm

33. GERARD TERBORCH. 1617—1681. *Holland*
Portrait of a Lady. Early 1650s
Oil on canvas. 62×46 cm

38. REMBRANDT HARMENSZ VAN RIJN.
1606—1669. *Holland*

Portrait of Adriaen van Rijn (?). 1654

Signed and dated, top left: *Rembrandt 1654*
Oil on canvas. 74 × 63 cm

37. REMBRANDT HARMENSZ VAN RIJN.
1606—1669. *Holland*

Ahasuerus, Haman and Esther. 1660

Signed and dated, bottom left: *Rembrandt f 1660*
Oil on canvas. 73×94 cm

36. JURIAEN VAN STREECK. 1632—1687. *Holland*
Vanitas

Bottom left, a touched-up signature: *J v Streek f*
Oil on canvas. 98×84 cm

35. PIETER DE HOOCH. 1629—*c.* 1684. *Holland*
Morning of a Young Man
Oil on panel. 40×53 cm

34. PHILIPS KONINCK. 1619—1688. *Holland*
A View in Gelderland
Oil on canvas. 131×161 cm

39. REMBRANDT HARMENSZ VAN RIJN.
1606—1669. *Holland*
Portrait of an Elderly Woman. *C.* 1650
Signed and dated, top right: *Rembrandt f 165[...]*
Oil on canvas. 82×72 cm

40. PETER PAUL RUBENS.
1577—1640. *Flanders*
Bacchanal. *C.* 1615
Oil on canvas (transferred from panel). 91×107 cm

41. PETER PAUL RUBENS. 1577—1640. *Flanders*

The Apotheosis of the Archduchess Isabella. 1634

Inscribed above the entrance: *IN VERVMQ PARATVS EN VINCE;*
HIC VIR HIC EST [...]
Oil on panel, 68×70 cm

42. ANTHONY VAN DYCK. 1599—1641. *Flanders*
Portrait of Adriaen Stevens. 1629
Signed and dated, left, on the column: *Aet^S, 68. A^O 1629 Ant. van dijck. fe*
Oil on canvas. 110×93 cm

43. FRANS SNYDERS.
1579—1657. *Flanders*
Fish Shop
Signed, bottom right: *F. Snyders fecit*
Oil on canvas. 134×204 cm

44. JACOB JORDAENS. 1593—1678.
Flanders

A Satyr in a Peasant House. Early 1620s
Oil on canvas. 153×205 cm

48. BARTCLOMÉ ESTEBAN MURILLO.
1617—1682. *Spain*

Archangel Raphael and Bishop Domonte. After 1680
Oil on canvas. 211×150 cm

47. FRANCISCO DE ZURBARÁN. 1598—1664. *Spain*
The Infant Christ. 1635—1640s
Oil on panel. 42×27 cm

46. JAN SIBERECHTS 1627—c 1703. *Flanders*

Ford. 1669

Signed and dated in the centre, on the wagon-shaft: *J. Siberechts: 1669: f*
Oil on canvas. 94×116 cm

45. DAVID TENIERS THE YOUNGER. 1610—1690.
Flanders
Jester. *C.* 1650
Signed, bottom left: *D. Teniers F.*
Oil on canvas. 35×29 cm

49. ALESSANDRO MAGNASCO (called LISSANDRINO).
1667—1749. *Italy*
Nuns at the Refectory Table
Oil on canvas. 93×75 cm

50. GIUSEPPE MARIA CRESPI (called LO SPAGNUOLO).
1665—1747. *Italy*
The Holy Family. *C.* 1712
Oil on canvas. 248×192 cm

51. GIOVANNI BATTISTA TIEPOLO.
1696—1770. *Italy*
The Death of Dido. Sketch. 1757 (?)
Oil on canvas. 40×63 cm

52. MICHELE GIOVANNI
MARIESCHI. 1710—1743. *Italy*
View of the Grand Canal in Venice
Oil on canvas. 130×195 cm

53. FRANCESCO GUARDI. 1712—1793. *Italy*
Courtyard in Venice. *C.* 1770

Oil on canvas. 38×26 cm

54. NICOLAS POUSSIN. 1594—1665. *France*
Satyr and Nymph. C. 1630
Oil on canvas. 77.5×62.5 cm

55. NICOLAS POUSSIN. 1594—1665. *France*

Landscape with Hercules and Cacus. *C.* 1660

Oil on canvas. 156×202 cm

56. NICOLAS POUSSIN. 1594—1665. *France*

Rinaldo and Armida. Early 1630s

Oil on canvas. 95×133 cm

57. CLAUDE GELLÉE (CLAUDE LORRAIN).
1600—1682. *France*
Battle on the Bridge. 1655
Signed, inscribed and dated, bottom right, on a stone: *Claudio G... V Romae 1655*
Oil on canvas. 100×137 cm

58. ANTOINE WATTEAU. 1684—1721. *France*
The Bivouac. *C.* 1710
Oil on canvas. 32×45 cm

59. HYACINTHE RIGAUD. 1659—1743. *France*
Portrait of the Writer Bernard le Bovier de Fontenelle. C. 1720—30
Oil on canvas. 54×44 cm

61. FRANÇOIS BOUCHER. 1703—1770. *France*
Hercules and Omphale. 1730s
Oil on canvas. 90×74 cm

60. ANTOINE QUILLARD. 1701—1733. *France*
The Pastoral. 1730s
Oil on canvas. 72×91.5 cm

Daubigny 1858

69. THOMAS LAWRENCE. 1769—1830.
England

Portrait of Sally Siddons. 1790s
Oil on canvas. 40×34 cm

70. CHARLES FRANÇOIS DAUBIGNY.
1817—1878. *France*

Morning. 1858
Signed and dated, bottom right: *Daubigny 1858.*
Oil on panel. 29×47 cm

68. JOHN CONSTABLE. 1776—1837.
England
View of Highgate from Hampstead Heath. *C.* 1830
Oil on cardboard. 24×30 cm

67. CASPAR DAVID FRIEDRICH. 1774—1840.
Germany
Mountainous Landscape
Oil on canvas. 45×58 cm

66. EUGÈNE DELACROIX. 1798—1863. *France*

After a Shipwreck. 1847

Signed, bottom left: *Eug. Delacroix*
Oil on canvas. 36×52 cm

65. THÉODORE GÉRICAULT. 1791—1824. *France*
Study of a Male Model. *C.* 1810—11
Oil on canvas. 64×53 cm

64. ANTOINE JEAN GROS. 1771—1835. *France*
Equestrian Portrait of Prince Boris Yusupov. 1809
Signed and dated, bottom left: *Gros. 1809*
Oil on canvas. 321×266 cm

63. JACQUES-LOUIS DAVID. 1748—1825. *France*

Andromache Laments the Death of Hector. 1783

Signed and dated, bottom left: *L. David 1783*
Oil on canvas. 58×43 cm

62. JACQUES-LOUIS DAVID. 1748—1825. *France*
Portrait of Ingres as a Young Man (?)
Oil on canvas. 54×47 cm

71. NARCISSE DIAZ DE LA PEÑA. 1807—1876. *France*

The Approaching Storm. 1871

Signed and dated, bottom left: *N. Diaz 71*
Oil on panel. 21×30 cm

72. GUSTAVE COURBET. 1819—1877. *France*

The Sea. 1867

Signed and dated, bottom right: *G. Courbet 67*.
Oil on canvas. 103×126 cm

73. JEAN FRANÇOIS MILLET. 1814—1875.
France

Women Gathering Brushwood (Charcoal Burners). 1850s

Signed, bottom right: *J. F. Millet*
Oil on canvas. 37×45 cm

77. EUGÈNE BOUDIN. 1824—1893. *France*
On the Beach. Trouville. 1871
Signed and dated, bottom left: *E. Boudin 1871.*
Inscribed, bottom right: *Trouville.*
Oil on panel. 19×46 cm

76. JULES BASTIEN-LEPAGE. 1848—1884.
France
Village Love. 1882
Signed and dated, bottom left: *J. Bastien-Lepage Damvillers*
Oil on canvas. 194×180 cm

75. PIERRE PUVIS DE CHAVANNES. 1824—1898.
France
Poor Fisherman. Sketch. 1879
Signed and dated, bottom right: *P. Puvis de Ch. 79*
Oil on canvas 66×91 cm

74. JEAN-BAPTISTE CAMILLE COROT.

1796—1875. *France*

Morning in Venice. 1834

Signed, bottom right: *VENTE Corot*
Oil on canvas. 27.5×40 cm

78. CLAUDE MONET. 1840—1926. *France*

The Boulevard des Capucines in Paris. 1873

Signed and dated, bottom: *Claude Monet 73*
Oil on canvas. 61×80 cm

79. CLAUDE MONET. 1840—1926. *France*

Haystack at Giverny. 1884—89

Signed, bottom left: *Claude Monet*

Oil on canvas. 64×87 cm

80. CAMILLE PISSARRO. 1830—1903. *France*

Avenue de l'Opéra in Paris. 1898

Signed and dated, bottom right: *C. Pissarro 98*
Oil on canvas. 65×82 cm

81. ALFRED SISLEY. 1839—1899. *France*
The Skirts of the Forest of Fontainebleau. 1885

Signed and dated, bottom right: *Sisley. 85*
Oil on canvas. 60×73 cm

82. PIERRE AUGUSTE RENOIR. 1841—1919. *France*

In the Garden. Under the Trees of the Moulin de la Galette. 1875
Signed, bottom right: *Renoir*
Oil on canvas. 81×65 cm

83. PIERRE AUGUSTE RENOIR. 1841—1919. *France*

Girls in Black. Early 1880s

Signed, bottom right: *AR*

Oil on canvas. 81×65 cm

84. EDGAR DEGAS 1834—1917. *France*
Dancer Posing for a Photographer. 1870s
Signed, bottom right: *degas*
Oil on canvas. 65×50 cm

85. EDGAR DEGAS. 1834—1917. *France*
Blue Dancers. *C.* 1899
Signed, top left: *degas*
Pastel on paper. 64×65 cm

86. VINCENT VAN GOGH. 1853—1890. *Holland*
Landscape at Auvers after the Rain. 1890
Oil on canvas. 72×90 cm

87. VINCENT VAN GOGH. 1853—1890. *Holland*
Portrait of Dr Rey. 1889
Signed, inscribed and dated, bottom right: *Vincent Arles 89*
Oil on canvas. 64×53 cm

88. PAUL GAUGUIN. 1848—1903. *France*

Café at Arles. 1888

Signed and dated, twice — on the table, bottom right, and on the billiard-table:
P. Gauguin 88
Oil on canvas. 72×92 cm

89. PAUL GAUGUIN. 1848—1903. *France*

Are You Jealous? 1892
Signed and dated, bottom centre: *P. Gauguin 92*
Inscribed, bottom left: *Aha oe feii?*
Oil on canvas. 66×89 cm

90. PAUL GAUGUIN. 1848—1903. *France*

Self-portrait

Signed, bottom left: *P. Go*
Oil on canvas. 46×38 cm

93. PAUL CÉZANNE.
1839—1906. *France*
Still Life with Peaches and Pears.
1888—90
Oil on canvas. 61×90 cm

94. MAURICE DENIS. 1870—1943. *France*

At the Seaside. The Green Beach. 1909
Signed and dated, bottom left: *Maurice Denis 1909*
Oil on canvas. 97×180 cm

95. JEAN ÉDOUARD VUILLARD. 1868—1940. *France*

In the Room. 1904

Signed, bottom left: *E. Vuillard*
Oil on cardboard. 50×77 cm

96. PIERRE BONNARD. 1867—1947. *France*
Summer in Normandy. 1908 (?)
Signed. bottom right: *Bonncrd*
Oil on canvas. 114×128 cm

97. HENRI ROUSSEAU. 1844—1910. *France*
Jaguar Attacking a Horse. 1910
Signed, bottom right: *Henri Rousseau*
Oil on canvas. 90×116 cm

98. PAUL SIGNAC. 1863—1935. *France*

Sandy Seashore. 1890

Signed and dated, bottom left: *P Signac 90*
Oil on canvas. 65×81 cm

99. MAURICE UTRILLO. 1883—1955. *France*

Rue de Mon-Cenis. *C.* 1914—19

Signed, bottom right: *Maurice Utrillo V.*
Oil on canvas. 48×63 cm

100. EDVARD MUNCH. 1863—1944. *Norway*
White Night. Before 1903
Signed, bottom right: *E. Munch*
Oil on canvas. 83×73 cm

101. IGNACIO ZULOAGA. 1870—1945. *Spain*

Self-portrait

Signed, bottom left: *I. Zuloaga*
Oil on canvas. 76×65 cm

102. ALBERT MARQUET. 1875—1947. *France*
Notre-Dame in Winter. 1908
Signed, bottom left: *marquet*
Oil on canvas. 65×81 cm

103. MAURICE DE VLAMINCK. 1876—1958. *France*
Landscape at Auvers. 1924
Signed, bottom right: *Vlaminck*
Oil on canvas. 45×55 cm

104. ANDRÉ DERAIN. 1880—1954. *France*
Table by a Window. 1912 (?)
Signed on the reverse: *A. Derain*
Oil on canvas. 128×79 cm

105. ANDRÉ DERAIN. 1880—1954. *France*
The Castle (New Castle at La Roche-Guyon). *C.* 1910
Signed on the reverse: *A. Derain*
Oil on canvas. 66×87 cm

106. HENRI MATISSE. 1869—1954. *France*
Fruit and Bronze. 1910
Signed and dated, bottom centre: *Henri Matisse 1910*
Oil on canvas. 90×118 cm

107. HENRI MATISSE. 1869—1954. *France*
View from the Window. Tangier. Part of
the Moroccan triptych. 1912
Oil on canvas. 115×80 cm

108. HENRI MATISSE. 1869—1954. *France*
Zorah on the Terrace. Part of the Moroccan triptych. 1912
Oil on canvas. 116×100 cm

109. HENRI MATISSE. 1869—1954. *France*
Entrance to the Casbah. Part of the Moroccan triptych. 1912
Oil on canvas. 116.5×80 cm

110. CORNELIS (KEES) VAN DONGEN.
1877—1968. *Holland*

Spanish Woman. *C.* 1910

Signed, top right: *van Dongen*
Oil on canvas. 46×39 cm

111. GEORGES ROUAULT. 1871—1958.
France
Bathing in the Lake. 1907
Signed and dated, bottom right: *G. Rouault 1907*
Watercolour and pastel on paper. 65×96 cm

112. PABLO PICASSO. 1881—1973. *Spain*
Portrait of the Poet Jaime Sabartés. 1901
Signed, top left: *Picasso*
Oil on canvas. 82×66 cm

113. PABLO PICASSO. 1881—1973. *Spain*
Spanish Woman from Mallorca. 1905
Signed, bottom left: *Picasso*
Tempera, watercolour and gouache on cardboard. 67×51 cm

114. PABLO PICASSO. 1881—1973. *Spain*
Girl on a Ball. 1905
Signed, bottom right: *Picasso*
Oil on canvas. 147×95 cm

115. PABLO PICASSO. 1881—1973. *Spain*
Queen Isabeau. 1909
Oil on canvas. 92×73 cm

116. ROCKWELL KENT. 1882—1971.
The United States of America
Spring Fever. 1908
Signed, bottom right: *Rockwell Kent.*
Oil on canvas. 87×112 cm

117. FERNAND LÉGER. 1881—1955. *France*

Woman Reading a Book (Portrait of Nadia Léger). 1949

Signed and dated, bottom right: *F. Leger 49*
Oil on canvas. 92×73 cm

118. RENATO GUTTUSO. 1912—1987. *Italy*

Man Crossing a Square. 1958

Signed, bottom right: *Guttuso*
Inscribed and dated on the reverse: *Guttuso "uomo che cammina" '58*
Oil on canvas. 195×165 cm

119. DECHKO UZUNOV. Born 1899. *Bulgaria*

Protest
Signed, bottom right: Д Уз
Oil on canvas. 89.2×135.5 cm

120. CORNELIU BABA. Born 1906. *Romania*
Still Life. 1967
Signed and dated, bottom right: *Baba* (illegible) *67*
Oil on canvas. 89.5×70 cm

КАРТИННАЯ ГАЛЕРЕЯ "АВРОРЫ"

**ГОСУДАРСТВЕННЫЙ МУЗЕЙ ИЗОБРАЗИТЕЛЬНЫХ ИСКУССТВ
ИМЕНИ А. С. ПУШКИНА, МОСКВА. ЖИВОПИСЬ**

Альбом (на английском языке)

Издательство „Аврора", Ленинград, 1992
Изд. № 2125
ПО „Типография имени Ивана Федорова"
Printed and bound in Russia